FREEDOM FAITH AND THE FUTURE

Michael Ramsey
Archbishop of Canterbury

WIPF *&* STOCK · Eugene, Oregon

Wipf and Stock Publishers
199 W 8th Ave, Suite 3
Eugene, OR 97401

Freedom, Faith, and the Future
By Ramsey, Arthur Michael
Copyright©1970 SPCK
ISBN 13: 978-1-60899-820-3
Publication date 7/9/2010
Previously published by SPCK, 1970

Preface

This book has as its background two of the passionate concerns which are felt today by many of the younger generation.

There is the concern for freedom. This is seen in the dislike of accepting beliefs or codes of conduct on the ground of tradition or authority and in the desire to thrash out convictions for oneself. It is seen also in the hatred of seeing other people subjected to persecution or discrimination on grounds of belief or opinion or race or colour. But while it is easy to see what are the things we want to be free *from*, it is harder to see what are the things we should be free *for*. It is this issue which Christianity poses, and this book tries to explore it.

Alongside the concern about freedom there is the concern about human suffering. Those who denigrate the young people of today in vague and sweeping terms do not always know that amongst them there is a practical concern about the suffering of their fellow men and women greater perhaps than in any previous generation. This is seen in an eagerness to help those who are hungry or homeless or underprivileged in our own and in other countries. Here too some baffling questions arise about ends and meanings. When people are freed from poverty, what then? The more affluent countries have their own ghastly frustrations and perversities. We find ourselves asking what kind of society is man's goal. Is the true goal of man definable or attainable in terms of this life alone?

The discussion of these questions involves us in theology—the Christian belief in God. Nothing makes belief in God harder than does the phenomenon of suffering itself with the terrible dilemmas which it poses. I try in this book to show how Christ helps us to face this problem, and how his answer throws light not only upon man but upon what it means for God to be God.

These four discourses were given in the University Church in Cambridge in the Lent term of 1970. By a new and interesting arrangement the University Sermons were moved from their usual time in the afternoon and attached to the evening service. I would express my gratitude to the University of Cambridge for honouring me with the office of Hulsean Preacher, and to Dr Owen Chadwick, the Vice-Chancellor, and Hugh Montefiore, at the time Vicar of Great St Mary's, for their kindness and encouragement.

July 1970   MICHAEL CANTUAR:

Contents

The glorious liberty
of the children of God

Romans 8.21, R.S.V.

1 Freedom

I

I cannot doubt that everyone who is present here is likely to have much concern about freedom in one way or another. We feel a sense of outrage at some of the denials of freedom in the contemporary world. We believe that there should be freedom for people to express their opinions, to practise whatever religion they choose or none, to uphold whatever ideology or philosophy they choose or none. We are outraged when we meet discrimination on grounds of race or colour, and we believe that it should have no place in any human community. We hate to see people robbed of freedom to fulfil their lives through poverty or hunger. To these concerns, which belong to our common humanity, there has been added in recent years, not least within the university populations in the West, a passionate demand to make decisions, including ethical decisions, without the pressures of authority or tradition. We wish to decide for ourselves: we will not be told what we are to do.

But what does freedom really mean? We are free to discuss it. So let us do so. The inclination of all of us is to think that a person's freedom is his ability to do what he chooses as and when he chooses to do it. But when we put this idea of freedom to the test we find very soon that it runs into frustrations. Thus you can on Monday do what you like as and when you like to do it, and again on

Tuesday, and again on Wednesday, and perhaps again on Thursday. Then, by the time Friday comes, you may find there is something you had ardently wanted to do and yet you cannot do it because the distractions of the previous days have undermined your power to do what you had in fact regarded as a major purpose. In a word, you were not as free as you supposed: your freedom can be in conflict with your freedom. The initial definition of freedom is damaged under the blows of day-to-day experience.

So we are drawn to try another definition of freedom. Here is one. "My freedom is not my power to do what I choose as and when I choose it. My freedom is rather my ability to choose an end or a goal and to unify my faculties in the consistent pursuit of that end or goal." Does that definition commend itself, at least as making more sense than the one with which we began? But notice these aspects of it. It is a freedom which may need restraints if it is to thrive and grow. These restraints may be suggested to me by myself, or they may be suggested by the community as it collectively pursues a freedom shared by its members, for it is no freedom when one person's freedom invades that of someone else. Next, it is not only a freedom from something, it is a freedom *for* something. Third, it is freedom for a personality to become its own true self, not only to be itself as it now is but to realize itself in maturity.

So far our empirical inquiry has led us, and has set us querying the popular idea of freedom and probing through experience towards something deeper. Now I turn to Christianity. Does its teaching throw light on our problem? We look first at the historical figure of Jesus and the nature of his freedom. Then we look at the philosophy of freedom, derived from Jesus, as Christianity presents it.

II

Jesus the free man, Jesus the embodiment of freedom: that is one of the ways in which he has caught the reverent attention of many. Recently several writers about Jesus in history have dwelt upon this aspect of him. Taking first as our authority the records in the first three Gospels, I ask what aspects of the freedom of Jesus stand out in the story of his life.

Jesus is free from the rule of tradition. He sets it aside, often drastically. You remember the reiterated antithesis in the Sermon on the Mount, "You have heard that it was said by those of old time, but I say unto you ..."

Jesus is free from the dominance of conventions. He consorts with those whom respectable society thought it right to shun: prostitutes, profiteers, hated financial agents of an alien empire. He shocked people by this freedom.

Jesus is free from the pressure of life's circumstances. Let me explain. He feels the tragedies of the world around him with intense sensitivity; he shares, he bears the sorrows of his fellows, he is plunged deep into the waters of human calamity. Yet there is in him an inward peace, a serenity, which seems to belong to another world. This is a very significant part of the freedom of Jesus.

Jesus is free from the dominance of the contemporary. He is not one who in rejecting old traditions is ruled by the current enthusiasms of his contemporaries. He is not caught into contemporary movements, the moralism of the Pharisees, or the otherworldliness of the apocalyptists,

11

or the ascetic withdrawal of the Essenes, or the revolutionary aims of the Zealots. Free from his own age, he seems timeless in his appeal and authority.

Beneath these freedoms of Jesus there is an underlying secret. He is free from someone and free for someone. He is free from self, and free for God.

How does this characteristic appear in the story? It appears in a blending of authority and self-effacement. Jesus wields a tremendous authority, and he speaks and acts in a way which implies tremendous claims. He forgives sins in God's name, he claims to embody the kingdom or reign of God in his own words and actions, he links the kingdom or reign of God with a personal allegiance to himself, he inaugurates a new divine–human covenant on the basis of his own death, he will be the one in whose presence men will one day be judged. These are claims indeed. Yet in the midst of this majestic authority he is effacing himself, he is making himself as nothing; for his centre is not in himself, his centre is in Another, in the one whom he calls "Father". The self is free from self because it is free *into* another, the Father, God.

How is this apparent? It is seen in the attitude of thankfulness, gratitude, praise, which lifts the self out of the self: the attitude of the worshipper. It is seen in the continual absorption into the Father's purposes and designs: it is meat and drink for Jesus to be making those purposes and designs his own. It is seen in obedience to what Jesus knows to be the Father's commands, right through from the scene in the Temple when as a boy Jesus said, "I must be about my Father's business", to the scene in the garden of Gethsemane when Jesus cries in an agony of prayer, "Father, if it be possible let this cup pass from me; nevertheless, not what I will but what thou wilt be done". These are the media of a freedom from self into God.

So far our picture has come from the first three Gospels. When we turn to the fourth Gospel we see the life of Jesus interpreted in a portrait in which one of the key words is glory. Jesus reveals glory. But he does not glorify himself, he looks to the Father's glory, he effaces himself in order to give glory to the Father. He has indeed glory, but no independent glory for himself, because the essence of glory is self-giving love, to live in another and for another.

Such is the freedom of Jesus. Today despite the decline in religion and the widespread rejection of dogmatic Christianity, and despite the dislike of looking back to a past century for guidance, the figure of Jesus goes on haunting the thoughts and consciences of men. The secret is his freedom, but a freedom far different from that which men easily understand.

It is from the freedom of Jesus as known in history that Christianity draws its doctrine or philosophy of freedom. Christianity affirms that in God alone is perfect freedom, the consistent self-realization of One who is utterly good, righteous, and wise, the "I am that I am". God is free. And God has created the human race in his own likeness with the design that his human creatures, endowed with the rudiments of free will, may through their right use of it come to share in his own freedom in sonship. They will attain this freedom in the knowledge of God, in the doing of his purposes, in self-forgetful love towards one another in mutual service and towards him in contemplation, with him as their centre, their goal, and their *glory*. So it is that the ancient prayer speaks of God as one whom to serve is true freedom, *cui servire regnare;* and the apostle Paul describes the goal of the created

13

universe as the glorious freedom of the children of God.

In Jesus we see not only the free man of all time but the embodiment of divine freedom, for in his life God discloses himself completely and uniquely in time and history. When in his words and actions Jesus "glorifies" the Father and knows that the Father "glorifies" him— not least in the self-effacement of his death—there is revealed the character of eternal deity, love, glory, freedom. In Jesus we see not only what it means for man to be free but also what it means for God to be God.

Not surprisingly, Christians see Jesus not only as the image of what freedom is but as the source of freedom to us. This is described in a sentence in the Fourth Gospel: "If you continue in my word, you are truly my disciples, and you will know the truth, and the truth will make you free" (John 8. 31–2). It is a relation of close personal allegiance to Jesus, mediated by the reading of the Gospels, by prayer, by sacrament, by exposure to the impact of Jesus upon us which is called "grace". Learning from this relationship to Jesus the "truth", about God as our creator and saviour and about ourselves as creatures and sinners, we are set in the path which leads to the freedom of mature sonship. The truth shall make us free.

When the apostle Paul speaks of the "glorious freedom of the children of God" he is thinking of the final goal of heaven in which freedom is perfectly realized. In all our thinking and acting about freedom we bear in mind that final reference. The different aspects of freedom which we cherish and realize in this life are fragmentary anticipations of the freedom which is heaven itself. Yet the freedom derived from Jesus begins now. It is here, real and creative.

III

Our present concerns about freedom upon the human scene are not abrogated by the Christian conception on which we have been thinking. Rather are those concerns reaffirmed in their urgency. As Christians we must be the sworn foes of persecution, of arbitrary imprisonment, of racial discrimination, of crippling poverty and hunger. We shall throw ourselves into these causes of freedom in the name of Christ; and our Christian discipleship will be tested by our practical concern for our fellows. But we shall be aware that while these issues are easily stated in terms of freedom *from*, awkward questions arise when we go on to questions about freedom *for*. History shows that communities can be well fed, prosperous, and highly cultured, liberal and democratic as well, enjoying a host of the freedoms we care about, and yet be a prey to selfishness, self-indulgence, indecent luxury, domestic unhappiness, and—so far from being mentally free—can be at the mercy of contemporary blasts of sentiment and folly. We know what we want to free men from. Do we know what we want to free men for?

So our striving as Christians for the freedoms which most palpably stir our feelings is always in the context of the more radical and revolutionary issue of the freeing of man from self and for the glory of God, a freedom whose goal is heaven and whose reflection is in a thousand actions here and now. Here each one of us starts with himself and his own need for freedom from self and into God. You can shout and protest on behalf of freedom on this issue and that, and yet be evading the Divine Protest which is addressed to each of us. Seven hundred years before Christ the Divine Protest was addressed by the prophet Micah, in the midst of social evils not unlike those of our own time:

> Hear what the Lord says: Arise, plead your case before the mountains, and let the hills hear your voice. Hear, you mountains, the controversy of the Lord, and you enduring foundations of the earth; for the Lord has a controversy with his people... He has showed you, O man, what is good; and what does the Lord your God require of you but to do justice, and to love kindness, and to walk humbly with your God?
> *Micah 6. 1–2, 8*

Hear too the Divine Protest as St John gives it to each of us:

> If we say that we have no sin, we deceive ourselves, and the truth is not in us. If we confess our sins, he is faithful and just, and will forgive our sins and cleanse us.
> *1 John 1. 8–9*

That is where our own service of freedom begins. Hear, above all, the Divine Protest in the words of Jesus:

> Unless you turn, and become like little children, you will never enter the kingdom of heaven.   *Matthew 18.3*

> Blessed are the pure in heart, for they shall see God.
> *Matthew 5.8*

We who are Christians have an extraordinarily difficult mission: to care for those aspects of human freedom which are obvious to the enlightened conscience and to join with all others, Christians or non-Christians, men of any religion or no religion, in contending against those injustices which so palpably mar freedom upon the human scene—and at the same time to keep before ourselves and others the truth about freedom of which we have been thinking, that its enemy is self and its goal is the glory of God. Without that context our striving for freedom may become a perpetually revolving circle, as history has often shown.

I end with a reference to two aspects of freedom which Christians are called upon to enjoy and to extend.

There is the intellectual freedom of the Christian. It may startle you to hear this mentioned, because Christians and Churches have sometimes been guilty of the most flagrant violation of intellectual freedom and resistance to new discoveries. Yet I believe that when these things happen it is a falling away from the truth and freedom of Christ, and I believe that rightly used the Christian creed is a means of intellectual liberty. To believe, freely and by your own conviction, that God is our creator, that Jesus in his life and death and rising shows what it means for God to be God, that our goal is to become like him —to believe *that* is to accept indeed a certain yoke of specific belief, yet how liberating it can be. It frees you into the large room of the family of Christ's followers across the ages. There is a timelessness about such a faith. It is not first-century or sixteenth-century or twentieth-century. It can free you from one of the most horrible of tyrannies, the dominance of the contemporary.

There is also for the Christian the freedom from the pressure of life's circumstances which we saw to be a part of Jesus' own freedom. A Christian true to his name will be keenly sensitive to the tragedies of the world and the faults and sorrows of other people, as well as his own sins. He will feel, he will share, he will bear. Yet he will find a serenity coming from a source beyond himself, and unaccountable from the world's own circumstances, the inner peace of which Jesus spoke to the disciples on the night before the Crucifixion: "Peace I leave with you, my peace I give unto you; not as the world gives give I unto you." The Christian expects storms: in a wonderful way Christ is there with him.

17

Amidst the strains and conflicts of our quest for freedom we can recall the scene of the crucifixion of Jesus. In that scene those who brought about the death of Jesus believed that they were acting in their freedom and that Jesus was stripped of his freedom in being done to death. In fact, they all were fast bound in the compulsive actions of prejudice and selfishness, and in Jesus alone true freedom is seen—for the way of freedom is to die to live, to give self away so that self may be realized. That is the freedom of the sons of God.

*The sufferings of this present time
are not worth comparing with the
glory that is to be revealed to us*

Romans 8.18, R.S.V.

2 Faith

I

Is God credible? I ask you to discuss one amongst the formidable considerations which cause some to say "no". The one which I choose is the suffering in the world. I do so for two reasons. One is that here the credibility of God is questioned with a special poignancy. The other is that here we face not only whether God is credible but what in the Christian sense it means for God to be God.

The problem is one which ethical monotheism has always had haunting its doorstep. It asserts that God is one, loving and omnipotent, and meanwhile the world is a scene of appalling suffering. Which of us cannot be sensitive to the cries heard again and again in history: "Why has God allowed this?" "I may believe in God, but if I believe in him, how can I ever forgive him?" "It's God they ought to crucify instead of you and me."

We start by saying that a vast volume of human suffering is the result of human sinfulness and folly, the recurring unkindness of man to man, an unkindness which has come to be entangled into the complex structures of the world's life. Man has misused his freedom and lent himself and his powers to pride and greed and self-aggrandizement. Individuals, groups, nations, designed to serve one another and to use the earth's resources for the good of one another and for the glory of God, have chosen instead to aggrandize themselves at the expense of others.

It is this perversion of human life which theologians call the Fall; and the story of Adam and Eve in the Book of Genesis, incredible as an historical story, is a symbolic parable of the truth that man is free and responsible and has misused his freedom with catastrophic results. If it be asked whether the creator could not make a good and happy world without these horrible possibilities, there is the answer that it is hard to see how there can be a moral universe, a universe in which ethics have meaning and love and virtue have existence, unless there is the free choice of the creature and the risks inherent in that. Man chooses to follow impulses of self-centredness instead of the way of unselfishness, the way which is ultimately "die to live" to which conscience prompts him.

We start therefore with the volume of human suffering which human selfishness, fear, laziness, and insensitivity have caused, with the unkindness which is now woven into the fabric of human affairs. The biblical writers summed up this state of affairs by saying that the world is "under judgement": a world whose actions bring calamity upon itself. To a world under judgement the biblical writers go on to say "repent", and repent means both "turn" and "be sorry". The share of any one of us in the total volume of the world's estrangement from God's goodness may seem to be infinitesimally small. But nothing is infinitesimally small in our relation to one who loves us and cares for us infinitely, and it is for each of us to repent —repent of that little area of the world's life for which he is responsible. Only thus, by putting myself right with God, am I likely to have the knowledge of him which can lead me to any understanding of this problem. "If we say that we have no sin, we deceive ourselves and truth is not in us. If we repent God is faithful and will forgive our sins."

II

Yet there is also the vast amount of suffering which seems attributable to no human fault or cause. There can be none of us whose heart has not sometimes been broken by tragedies through accidents of nature or through sickness or disease which bring pain and grief. There have been speculative explanations, like the theory of a demonic force working in nature in rebellion against the creator's good purpose; but none of these explanations, however plausible, are proved or revealed. But there are two considerations which experience has found to bring some comfort and conviction when the problem agonizingly presses on us.

One consideration is that in the midst of apparently insoluble suffering some of the most heroic of human qualities have been seen: a seemingly supernatural patience, courage, sympathy, gentleness, a power to turn pain to good account such as the biblical word "transfigure" describes. And when this is experienced we find that in the abyss of the problem of evil it is the problem of good which invades the scene and makes its own challenge.

The other consideration is this. As long as we are as a race collectively sinful and selfish, there would be little chance of our growing out of our sinfulness and selfishness if the world of nature were uniformly comfortable and free from accident. Because this world contains hazards we are discouraged from settling down with our horizons limited to it as if it were all, and we are spurred on in the path of unselfish brotherhood and in the hope of heaven beyond this life. At once I sense the protest that I am invoking heaven as a compensation for an insoluble problem. If so, I reply that heaven is in its essence a state of unselfish goodness and sacrificial love, no compensation for our frustrations but rather a fulfilment of those qualities as lived and practised in this world.

I claim no more than that those two considerations, which add up to no theoretical solution, have braced men and women to endure and to find God near to them in times of pain and sorrow. For the answer of faith we turn to the biblical writers. Their method is not to try to explain the problem or to explain it away, but somehow to carry it into the presence of God and to see what happens to it in that context. Prophets, psalmists, poets, dramatists like the author of the Book of Job, proclaimed in a crescendo of prophecies that God is one, God is righteous, God is loving, God is ruler, God is ruler of all, God is saviour, God is saviour of all; and the more they thus proclaimed the more exposed were they to sensitivity about the agonies of suffering. In sum, their answer was this. Do not argue, do not theorize, keep near to God, in nearness to him things become different. "I will hold me fast by God." That is the experience and the advice. "I will hold me fast by God." Keep near to him, and see what happens. That was the way of faith, and it is the way of faith still. "See what happens to you, and to the suffering, through God's nearness to you": it is a summons to a practical experience. But faith moves on to hope; and the men of faith in the Old Testament look forward, and they say: "Keep near to God. See what difference that makes. But also wait, God is going to act; look forward, God is going to do something." And the biblical writers use various kinds of imagery about what God is going to do: the imagery of the coming of the kingdom, the coming of the Messiah, the coming of the day of the Lord, the coming of God as deliverer.

What happened? The climax of the prophetic hope was the history of Jesus of Nazareth. Jesus came into Galilee as a prophet proclaiming that God's kingdom, that is God's reign or sovereignty, is here. It was, he taught, present in the righteousness which he expounded, a righteousness embodied in himself. It was present, he also taught, in the acts of power which he performed. Many of those acts of power were directed to the removal of human suffering. Christians see in these works of healing by Jesus the authority and sanction for all time for Christians to strive to remove suffering in every way that they can, whether by prayer and sacrament or by medical science or by both. But if men looked to Jesus for a straightforward programme of removing all suffering and substituting a painless world for a suffering world, they were disappointed; and they will be disappointed still. For at the heart of his message there is the call: repent, be sorry, turn to God and God's righteousness, become like little children in receiving his gifts of goodness. Suffering is hateful; men should be freed from it: but better learn righteousness and experience pain and sorrow than enjoy a painless world and continue in unrepenting selfishness.

We follow the story to its climax. So far from disappearing from the path of Jesus the forces of evil gathered strength, and it was clear that if he persisted in his mission those who hated his message and his claims would destroy him in death. But how did he view the death, terrible and ignominious, which lay in his path? Was it to be one more defeat of goodness, one more addition to the mountain of the problem of evil? No, it was to be, for Christianity, the secret of God's answer. Jesus taught the disciples, in the days before the final crisis, that though it would be wicked men who would perpetrate his death, it would be an event in which God's power, God's purpose, God's deliverance would be at work.

It was as lonely and ignominious as a death could be. Here is the earliest account of it, in the Gospel of St Mark:

> They crucified him, and divided his garments among them, casting lots for them, to decide what each should take.... And those who passed by derided him, wagging their heads, and saying, "Aha! ... save yourself, and come down from the cross." So also the chief priests mocked him to one another with the scribes, saying "He saved others; he cannot save himself. Let the Christ, the king... come down now from the cross, that we may see and believe." ... And when the sixth hour had come, there was darkness over the land until the ninth hour. And at the ninth hour Jesus cried with a loud voice, "Eloi, Eloi, lama sabachthani? ... My God, my God, why hast thou forsaken me?"
>
> *Mark 14. 24–33*

Jesus gave himself. He would not save himself. He gave himself to share in the deep darkness of a world sinful, black, estranged. But the apostles of Jesus came to believe that when Jesus died in this manner, giving himself and not saving himself, he was not contradicting the reign of God. Rather was he, the divine son, showing what the reign of God is like and how the reign of God comes, indeed what God himself is like. In the utter self-giving of Jesus in the desolation of his death there is the divine self-giving love, the very essence of deity. So St John, when he interprets the history in his own Gospel, does not hesitate to describe the death as *glory*. When Jesus dies we see the *glory* which is God's in all eternity, the glory of the self-giving love of the Triune God.

This is what Christianity, in its heart and its essence, is about. Carry the thought a little further.

Calvary was not a defeat which needed the Resurrection to cancel it or avenge it or reverse it. No, Calvary was love's victory, God's power, God's reign. The Resurrection came quickly to seal it, and to carry its effects onward into the subsequent centuries.

God is revealed in the event: the answer is given, the answer that in the suffering of the world God suffers, sharing, bearing, intimate with those who suffer if they will accept the intimacy which he offers to them. There is a traditional doctrine that God is "impassible". Am I denying that doctrine? Essentially, I think not so. Is not the essential meaning of that old doctrine that God is perfect and supreme, and that his perfection can never be injured or reduced? God is never to be pitied, he is never thwarted or frustrated. If he suffers it is with a difference. He suffers not as one who is frustrated but in a suffering which flows from the love which is perfect and victorious. "I have overcome the world."

Where then does our faith stand? We believe indeed that God is omnipotent and sovereign. But his is always the sovereignty of a self-giving, pain-bearing love. There is no other sovereignty in the universe. In the imagery of the Apocalypse the Lamb (sacrificial self-giving) is on the throne (sovereignty). There is no throne except the throne where the Lamb is, the throne of Calvary. *There* we begin to see meaning, purpose, sovereignty within the world, *there* we begin to see the path which we can follow through the jungle of our frightening experiences. Where we see acts of sacrifice and love in human lives, these are never "lost" or wasted. They are the way to the heart of God himself, and they are used within his purpose of the overcoming of evil.

III

If that is the Christian answer it is an answer which we can assert only if we are ready to give to it the commitment of our lives. The answer is not the answer of an intellectual scheme, but the answer of a commitment of the self, a turning from the way of selfishness to the way of Christ, the way of living through dying. Jesus, on the way to Jerusalem, depicted that way to James and John the sons of Zebedee in some very vivid metaphors, and said to them "Are you able?" (Matt. 20.22). That is the question put to us.

Living through dying is what faith means; it is what baptism means, it is what Holy Communion means; it defines the life to which every Christian is called. For the early Christians it quite often meant martyrdom, and martyrdom is always one of the norms of the Christian vocation. But whether in martyrdom or in other ways, the Christian is called to a life of dying to self, a life in which the centre is not the self but God and other people. That can indeed be joyful, with the joy of forgetting self in the service of God and humanity. But in so far as pride lingers in us the struggle with self will be painful, causing us sometimes to weep over our selfish folly. Yet as the self is dethroned the joy is real, and the life of those who die to self is described by Jesus as happy, joyful, blessed.

It is in this context that the Christian faces suffering. While his Christian faith may heighten rather than diminish his sensitivity to it he will draw from his faith something of a clue to follow. He will, in the following of Christ, devote himself to the removing of suffering from his fellows wherever possible, supporting every effort to reduce its causes and its incidence. But he will also recall the saying that while Christ strove to remove suffering

28

from others as if nothing could be made of it, when it came to him he accepted it as if everything could be made of it. He will be encouraged in this by the example of many men and women who have suffered in body and mind and through their nearness to Christ have shown a sympathy, a courage, a love, a patience, and indeed a joy which seem to come from another world. Indeed the "glory that shall be revealed" belongs not only to the bliss of heaven to which the apostle points as beyond "the sufferings of this present time"; it presses insistently upon the present world scene.

Last week we saw that the key to human freedom is *die to live*. Now we see also that *die to live* is the key to the meaning of God himself and the key to his credibility. Facing the appalling problem of human suffering we find that the answer which Christianity gives is an answer which uses that problem for the disclosure of what it means for God to be God. This is a faith which throws a flood of light upon our understanding of the world and of ourselves, but only when it has first led us to a commitment of our lives. The world remains very dark. Faith enables you to see where you are going, and to draw other people to walk with you guided by the lamp who is Jesus the Christ.

*Everyone doing the building
must work carefully.
For the foundation, nobody can
lay any other than the one
which has already been laid,
that is Jesus Christ.*

1 Corinthians 3. 10–11
JERUSALEM BIBLE

3 The Servant Church

"I believe in Jesus Christ; I would like to follow him. But I cannot do with the institution of the Church. Must we have it?" Many people speak thus. So we shall discuss this question.

I would first pose the problem in this way. Jesus Christ rose from the dead in order that his impact upon the human race should continue and grow until the end of time. That is what Christianity is about. He brings his grace, power, love, truth to bear upon human lives in each generation. But those who receive this impact can never do so as isolated units. Each of them depends on somebody who helps to make Christ known by speech, or writing, or influence. And those who are Christ's "agents" in this way must somehow be connected with him and with one another in their own generation and across the generations. In however simple, however rudimentary a way, the "institution" thus comes in sight. And there will always be the contrast between Christ himself and those who represent him to others.

From the beginning to be a Christian involved these three things: to profess a belief summed up in the formula "Jesus is Lord"; to follow an ethical mode of life described as "the way"; and to belong to a society. That society had its rite of initiation, the sacrament of baptism, and its rite of worship and fellowship through participation in the death and resurrection of Jesus, the sacrament of the Eucharist. There was in primitive Christianity a simplicity which tended to be obscured when Christianity became more involved in the world's cultural life, and an ethical dynamic and freshness which tended to be obscured when the Church grew older and staler.

Yet our problem was there already. It was very soon in Christian history that there appeared the scandals which occur when men and women who are called to be saints are not quite saintly enough and the name of Christ is blasphemed. St Paul's first letter to the Church of Corinth poses the issue. Here is a Church which shows the virtues of Christian conversion in a wonderful way: and yet there are seen worldliness, moral compromise, intellectual distortions, quarrels and divisions. The second letter to the same Church shows us a glimpse of the apostle's way of facing the agonizing situation. He sees it as a call to share in the suffering of Christ rather than to drift into a sense of grievance, and by his nearness to the suffering of Christ he finds the power of Christ to reconcile and to restore.

So throughout history Jesus is made known in a society which teaches about him, hands on the knowledge of him, brings men and women into fellowship with him; and at the same time often conceals him and misrepresents him. We know now the ways in which this happens. Churches can tie themselves up with contemporary cultures and so become static and lack mobility of response. Christians can substitute a love of the institution itself for a love of Christ whom the institution exists to serve. A kind of religious professionalism can replace the simplicity of the Christian way. Lopsided intellectual and spiritual interpretations, leading to crude partisanship, can creep in and distort truth and fellowship. There can be conventional

32

and insincere religion, sheltering from life's problems in a cosy religious security. How human these things are. No one of us who is a Christian is free from them. But the Church is both human and divine: human in its recurring scandals, divine because within it there is the risen Jesus and his Spirit. Hence the pages of Christian history are filled with both disasters and revivals. But when revivals happen the pattern of events has often been this, a pattern seen both in Israel of old and in the Church of the new covenant. First judgement falls on the members of the Church: it becomes what the prophets called "a hissing and a reproach". Then a remnant may remain faithful. And then the prayer is heard: "O Lord, I have heard the report of thee, and thy work, O Lord do I fear. . . . in the midst of the years make it known; in wrath remember mercy" (Habakkuk 3.2).

II

In the face of this we who are Christians, we who—whatever may be our degree of involvement in the "institution"—claim to represent Christ in the world, are challenged not to have a grievance but to repent. We are *all* under the judgement of the Lord of the Church, the judge and the healer of the Church. If you are the Archbishop of Canterbury your faults do much damage because of your representative position: you represent Christianity in a place of public exposure. But if you are not the Archbishop of Canterbury you none the less represent Christ: you are a part of the "total Christian thing". To repent is to be sorry, and to turn.

Turn where? We turn towards Christ. Just now there is one aspect of Christ which is being very prominently brought to our notice, and rightly. Christ is the servant. Christ serves. The Church is the servant. The Church must serve. Here is a clue for us to follow. We may start our rediscovery of it in the majestic words spoken at the Last Supper:

> The kings of the Gentiles exercise lordship over them; and those in authority over them are called benefactors. But not so with you; rather let the greatest among you become as the youngest, and the leader as one who serves. For which is the greater, one who sits at table or one who serves? Is not the one who sits at table? But I am among you as one who serves. *Luke 22. 25-7*

Here is the clue. Let the Church, let every Christian, throw aside worldliness, pride of status, pride of institution, and serve humanity: Christlike Christians and a Christlike Church.

But we need to look more deeply into what this means. Already the revival of the idea of the servant Church is bringing some misconceptions, not unlike those which appeared in connection with the ministry of Jesus. Serving the world can all too easily be taken to mean giving the world the things which it thinks it needs without challenging its assumptions about what those needs are. In this way the Church can try to commend itself as a kind of welfare society, advertising itself to the world on the world's own terms, instead of witnessing to the world's needs for a radical conversion of its ideas and for a knowledge of God's will which matters more than physical comfort. Jesus never served the world more drastically than when he died on the cross for its sake.

In the New Testament writings there are two distinct Greek words which are commonly translated "servant". The recognition of the difference between them is necessary for the right understanding of the problem.

34

The one word is *diakonos* or deacon, and the corresponding verb. It is the word used in the teaching of Jesus at the supper which I quoted. It is a *functional* word. It means one who does certain acts towards others, in particular one who waits at table. Jesus does not sit to be waited upon; he waits upon his followers. The implication of this for us Christians is plain and overwhelming. We are called to the urgent practical service of the needs of the community.

The other word is *doulos*. It is properly translated slave. It expresses not function but *relationship*: belonging to someone, being owned by someone, and in the context we are discussing the someone is God or Christ. It is strange that the *New English Bible*, perhaps through a lapse into a kind of donnish gentility, shrinks from the issue and translates the word as "servant". Slave is the meaning; no rights, no claims, but total possession by another. So St Paul is Christ's slave, yielding himself to a Christ-possessed existence; and we are God's slaves as utterly belonging to him. Of course the image does not exhaust the whole truth: we are God's sons and Christ's friends, and each image of itself is insufficient. But the image of *doulos* as slave speaks of that God-possession which belongs to our true relationship. "I come from God, I belong to God, I go to God." So the Church serves humanity by being itself God-centred, God-possessed, and witnessing that it is only through being possessed by God that mankind can find its true freedom.

The younger generations of Christians today are vividly aware of the truth contained in the first of the words, *diakonos*. There is a wholesome intolerance of any Christianity which does not express itself in outgoing service. Not for a moment should we wish this to be otherwise. But if the service of humanity is to touch humanity's inner crisis it will include the living out of the Godward relationship which the word *doulos* expresses. We serve humanity best when our meeting of practical needs in practical ways is unselfconsciously penetrated by our witness to God as the eternal goal of man's existence.

III

In the light of this consideration of the concepts of "servant" we can examine two of the tensions or conflicts which appear in contemporary Christianity.

There is the tension between cultus, prayer, organized religious practice as traditionally understood and works of practical service to humanity. There is among you, I well know, the passionate conviction that in the words of St James "pure religion and undefiled is this: to visit the fatherless and widows in their affliction"—and not only the fatherless and the widows but the homeless, the hungry, the sick in mind and body, the victims of persecution and injustice. With this conviction there often goes the suspicion that the whole business of prayer, pious practices, church services, contemplation, is a kind of hobby of remote religious culture. And the feeling comes that it may be right, in the name of Christianity itself to put this hobby aside and to give oneself to the service of the world in a kind of religionless self-abandon, trusting that this will be nearer to Christ than any entrenched pious security. What do we say to this contrast? I believe that there has indeed been in our Christian civilization a species of religious security which keeps the tragedies of the world at a distance and utterly distorts the image of the God who is the Father of Jesus and the creator of the world. The revulsion from this is laudable, and the revolt is understandable. Yet we Christians serve our fellows ill unless in the midst of our involvement with them we are witnessing to their need and our own need of that direct (call it "vertical" if you will) knowledge of God which demands quietness, contemplation, prayer, sacrament. Do not be afraid of the frankly otherworldly strain in Christianity. Do not be afraid of looking towards heaven, for heaven is the meaning of our existence as created in God's likeness for fellowship with him. And the quest of heaven is very far from being a pious escapism, inasmuch as the essence of heaven is selfless love, the same love which drives you to go without your dinner to help a family which has no food at all.

The other contrast is between Christian life and fellowship in the institutional forms handed down through the years and Christian life and fellowship in what are called "experimental" or "non-Church" forms. Now the essence of Christian fellowship, that is to say the life of the *ecclesia* or people of God, does not of necessity involve Gothic buildings, choirs and organs, pews and hassocks, the apparatus of ecclesiastical culture. It involves people, people united to Christ and to one another by the rites which he gave; and in the earliest years of Christianity the people met not in specialized buildings but in one another's houses. What are the essentials of a Church? To perpetuate the knowledge of Jesus by listening to his life and teaching and the apostolic witness to him, to recall Jesus in his ever-present sacrifice in the breaking of the bread, to praise the Father through him in the power of the Spirit, to practise fellowship, to serve the world, to draw people to Christ and help them on the way to heaven. There are those who do this in the framework of the institutional "culture" which has lasted through the centuries with its appeal to eye and ear and memory and imagination. There are those who do this in houses and colleges and streets and factories. But let one thing be clear. It is a mistake to call the latter "non-Church" Christianity, for the meaning of "Church" is essentially the *ecclesia*, the people themselves. The phrase "experimental Christianity" is more accurate and helpful. I have a feeling that one of the future tasks of Christian understanding and reconciling is going to be not between Catholic and Protestant Christianity so much as between "traditional" and "experimental" ways in many places. All of us who try to follow Christ must learn from one another with the humility which can listen as well as the candour which can speak.

IV

Christianity is Jesus Christ alive in the world, in the body whose members are his servants, slaves, brothers, friends, priests, and know that these images are only fragments of the truth and wonder of their relation to him. As we discover new ways of serving Christ and of expressing our Christian fellowship in the community around us, we shall find new and enhanced meaning in Christianity's central rite, for the sacrament of the Eucharist is for all time our sharing in Christ's body broken in death. If the faults and sins of Christians, including our own, and the failures of Christian institutions make us often feel that we are stumbling in the dark, we shall not be afraid. It is, after all, the darkness of Calvary and the light of Easter which are still the conditions of the Christian life. "Everyone doing the building must work carefully. For the foundation, nobody can lay any other than the one which has already been laid, which is Jesus Christ."

The God of Hope

Romans 15.13, R.S.V.

4 The Future

I

Christians have faith. Christians have love. They also have hope. But what do they hope for? What do you hope for as a Christian?

The first hope of every Christian is the hope of heaven: the first, the nearest, the most relevant of his hopes. Does that surprise you? Is heaven a possibility too far away for immediate thought? No, while heaven is commonly mentioned in theological schemes among the "Last Things" it is really among the first things. God created man in his own likeness, and man exists in order to have the most intimate relation with God that is possible; a relationship of fellowship and indeed friendship intermingled with awe and dependence. To give glory to God, in the biblical phrase, is to enjoy that fellowship, to come to reflect God's own character of outgoing love and humbly to have God and not one's self as the centre. There lies man's true status, true freedom, and true destiny. Heaven is man becoming what he exists in order to become. God loves every one of us with the infinity of his love, God loves you so greatly that he wants you to be with him for ever, enjoying all that he has to give you and giving back to him all that you can give. Heaven is near, intimate to the very meaning of our existence. In St Augustine's words, "we shall rest and we shall see, we

41

shall see and we shall love, we shall love and we shall praise, in the end which is no end".

This hope bears immediately upon our daily life now. It tells us of the infinite worth of every man, woman, and child we meet. It affects our attitude to a number of ethical questions, as the eternal value of a person matters more than immediate comfort or utility. More still, heaven is being anticipated in our daily experience. Every act of unselfish love, every reaching out towards God in desire for him, anticipates heaven. So since heaven is a clue to much that we are doing from day to day it is not surprising that St John describes eternal life as a life already beginning. Eternal life in the Johannine writings means not only life in the world-to-come but life that is already shared with God: "This is eternal life, that they know thee the only true God, and Jesus Christ whom thou hast sent" (John 17.3).

But what is our hope concerning this world in which we are now living? Certainly Christ encourages us to have hope concerning it. We are to pray, "thy kingdom come on earth", and so to hope that God's rule may become apparent in the world everywhere. Thus we hope to see races free from injustice to one another, for racial strife is a denial of the divine image in man. We hope to see nations so using the earth's resources and economic structures that all may have enough to eat instead of some being affluent while others starve. We hope to see war and the possibility of war banished. We hope to see family life everywhere secure and stable, happy and unselfish, with sex fulfilling its true use in lifelong marriage. We hope to see chastity, honesty, and compassion prevail. We hope to see these things happen as part of a deep reconciliation between man and God through Jesus Christ. We hope to see people brought everywhere into fellowship with God through him. In all this we hold in one our hope about earth and our hope of heaven. A Christian can scarcely separate these hopes as Jesus is the lord both of earth and heaven.

II

We need however to warn ourselves against a false view of how the kingdom of God comes in the world. In the latter part of the last century and in the early years of this it was often supposed by Christians in the West that by a kind of steady progression the world would become more Christian in belief, more civilized in behaviour, more mature in scientific achievements, more happy and more prosperous, all these forces moving together in steady ascent towards a kind of Utopia to be identified with the Kingdom of God. But it is impossible to find sanction in the New Testament for thinking that the Kingdom of God will come in that kind of way. Neither our Lord nor the apostles encourage us to expect a steady advance of the good and a steady regression of evil, still less an idea that this would go hand in hand with culture and prosperity. Rather does some of the language of the New Testament suggest an ever-intensifying conflict between the evil and the good, issuing in a costly victory by the way of the Cross. So it is that the hope of the apostolic writers is focused far less upon the coming of the reign of God as a state of things which can be described than upon the coming of Christ himself. It is upon *him* that the hope is focused. *He* will come into his own. He will come to us: we shall go to him. It is in Christ, for Christ, that we hope.

A few days ago the Vicar asked me whether we should sing tonight the old hymn of Charles Wesley, "Lo, he comes with clouds descending". I thought for half an hour before replying. The imagery of Jesus coming again upon the clouds is an imagery in which we do not literally believe; some of the early Christians did believe it literally, though to others it was parable and symbol. The imagery can mislead. But after a little reflection I said, "Yes, we will sing it". Why? The words express the hope that in a way beyond our imagining, in a way for which all imagery is inadequate, Jesus will come to us and we shall find ourselves with him. Whether in this world or out of this world we cannot understand, but we shall find and be found: in joy that we are with him, in grief that our sins wound him, as wound him they do.

This means *judgement*. When we speak about the "last judgement" we do not mean that a kind of law court is organized in heaven. We are speaking rather of the climax, of the point of "no return" in a process which is already happening. Judgement is with us now: "this is the judgement, that the light has come into the world, and men loved darkness rather than light, because their deeds were evil" (John 3.19). By the presence of Jesus in the world, judgement happens. We are free; free to be selfish, free to wound the love of Jesus, free to separate ourselves from him, free to make a hell of our existence now and free finally to choose a hell of stewing in our own selfish juice. The judgement now happening for each of us can run on to a point of no return. Those of us who think we have known Christ may find that he disowns us because our lives have been a betrayal of him. Some who have never known Christ in this life (and may it not be *our fault* that some people have never known him?) may awake to discover that in their acts of compassion to sufferers they were serving him without knowing him; and they will hear a voice, "You did not know it, but it was to me you did it".

Now the thought of divine judgement is intensified as we think of some of the urgent issues which the world is facing. In the matter which I now mention I speak as a learner, and I would urge all of you to be learners too. There is available to help us the recently published book by the Vicar of Great St Mary's, *The Question Mark*. How is man treating the world where he lives? The pollution of the land, the air, and the water, which together constitute man's daily environment, is becoming so vast and so dangerous that the survival of the human race may be threatened. The exploitation of nature in unthinking ways for short-term human advantages can endanger aspects of nature upon which man's healthy existence depends. You will be shocked and startled by some of the facts set out from responsible scientific sources in the book which I have mentioned, and in others contained in its bibliography. For instance, you may not have realized, as I certainly have not realized myself, how important is the existence of trees in plenty for the conserving of the resources of life; and yet there is a Sunday newspaper of which one single edition consumes 150 acres of forest land. Where does this end?

From the study of these matters two questions seem to be posed.

(1) What as Christians do we say about our duty to posterity? Is it right for a few generations of our race to use the world in ways which suit us without the most careful and anxious thought for generations in the future? Here we find the old doctrine of the worth of every man and woman in God's creation through the ages crying out

45

aloud. This doctrine may stretch our imaginations far into the future and make us ask whether it is for us to plan prosperity and to enjoy such affluence as we can without thought, and action, towards persons whose lives will be in God's far distant future.

(2) What as Christians do we believe about man's relations to nature? Are we free to exploit nature at will? What, for instance, of the abominations of factory farming? We are sent back to the classic doctrine of man and nature found in the eighth Psalm. The psalmist describes how man is given a lordship over nature, to rule it and to use it: a lordship which has grown in ways of which the psalmist never dreamed. But it is a lordship neither absolute nor arbitrary, but under God's own sovereignty and will. Man and nature are together parts of one whole pattern of creation, together serving the glory of God. It is for us to recapture this doctrine, to reaffirm it, and to learn how to apply it in the frighteningly complex world in which we live. Blind exploitation of nature can damage man's future "prospects"; far worse, it can damage man's spiritual life because it damages that which exists to be reverenced by him. Would that we could see again the sensitivity to nature which marked some of the greatest poetry of the past!

III

I draw this discourse to an end, and the series of discourses which you have followed very patiently. It is my theme that Christians can be sure of what they believe, and that the centre of their certainty is the death and resurrection of Jesus. Die to live: the losing of self so as to find self: that is the key to human *freedom*, the key to *faith*, the key to the *servant Church*, and the key to the *future*. In that faith I try to live, and in it I should like to be ready to die.

At every point of our theme the Christian concern for this world and its immediate problems has pressed itself upon us: at every point the otherworldly doctrine of Christianity has thrown its own light upon this.

I have a feeling that big changes may come in the ways in which Christians express their faith in intellectual terms. The lessons of history encourage us not to fear such changes, so long as in escaping the dominance of the past we take equal care to escape the dominance of the contemporary, and retain an eye for those kinds of Christian imagery which though old have a timeless power to reach over the passage of centuries. I have a feeling also that the ways in which Christian fellowship is expressed both within itself and in relation to society as a whole may see no less big changes. In both those ways to be a Christian may become an even more exciting adventure than in the past.

Amidst changes in the formulation of Christianity we want to be sure that we are holding to the unchanging essence of our faith. How can we be sure? What is the difference between Christianity and some substitute for it? The test is whether we hold firmly to the Passion and Resurrection of the Saviour. Keep in mind the Cross; and you will know the horridness of your sins and your need for forgiveness, and you will never substitute a facile humanism for the gospel. Keep in mind the Resurrection; and you will know that the goal is heaven and will never slip into a secularized religion. I expect you have ambitions. Most people have ambitions, and there are ambitions which it is right to have. But there is one ambition which Christ requires of us if we bear his name: the ambition of being near to him. "Truly, truly, I say to you, unless a grain of wheat falls into the earth and dies, it remains alone; but if it dies, it bears much fruit. . . . If any one serves me, he must follow me; and where I am, there shall my servant be also, if any one serves me, the Father will honour him" (John 12.24, 26).

www.ingramcontent.com/pod-product-compliance
Lightning Source LLC
Chambersburg PA
CBHW061756040426
42447CB00011B/2326